chips & dips

TARLA DALAL

India's # 1 Cookery Author

S&C
SANJAY & CO.
MUMBAI

Second Printing : 2007

Copyright © Sanjay & Co.

ISBN 10 : 81-89491-35-0

ISBN 13 : 978-8-189491-35-2

Price: Rs. 89/-

Published & Distributed by : **Sanjay & Company**

353/A-1, Shah & Nahar Industrial Estate, Dhanraj Mill Compound, Lower Parel (W), Mumbai - 400 013. INDIA.
Tel. : (91-22) 2496 8068 • Fax : (91-22) 2496 5876 • E-mail : sanjay@tarladalal.com

Printed by : **Minal Sales Agencies**, Mumbai

UK and USA customers can call us on :

UK : 02080029533 • USA : 213-634-1406

For books, Membership on **tarladalal.com**, Subscription for **Cooking & More** and Recipe queries
Timing : 9.30 a.m. to 7.00 p.m. (IST), from Monday to Saturday
Local call charges applicable

Recipe Research & Production Design	**Nutritionists**	**Photography**	**Designed by**
Arati Fedane	Nisha Katira	Jignesh Jhaveri	Satyamangal Rege
Umaima Abdulally	Sapna Kamdar		
Vibhuti Punjabi		**Typesetting**	**Copy Editing**
Ritika Rajpal	**Food Styling**	Adityas Enterprises	Janani Gopalakrishnan
	Shubhangi Dhaimade		

DISCLAIMER

While every precaution has been taken in the preparation of this book, the publishers and the author assume no responsibility for errors or omissions. Neither is any liability assumed for damages resulting from the use of information contained herein.

BULK PURCHASES

Tarla Dalal Cookbooks are ideal gifts. If you are interested in buying more than 500 assorted copies of Tarla Dalal Cookbooks at special prices, please contact us at 91-22-2496 8068 or email : sanjay@tarladalal.com

INTRODUCTION

Chips and Dips as the name suggests, provides an insight into the exciting world of chips and dips, and provides a collection of delectable dips and scrumptious chips for all food lovers, even the calorie-conscious ones!

Chips and Dips offers a fabulous variety of recipes with something for every food lover depending on your tastes and preferences, from extra-rich and savoury combos to amazingly low-fat and subtle choices. Inspired by a range of ethnic traditions, the recipes include old and new favourites for bean, vegetable, cheese, and lentil dips and unbeatably tasty chips to go with them. Served hot or cold, these irresistible snacks are sine qua non for entertaining, and compliment every party for every occasion.

More than being interesting appetisers, chips and dips can be seen as starters, as they go well with various alcoholic and non-alcoholic beverages in parties and other social gatherings. These are small bite-sized titbits, which tease rather than appease your appetite, leaving you craving for more.

What makes chips and dips a universal favourite among hosts and guests alike is the fact that they are not only tasty but also very easy to make and serve. Most of them can be made in large volumes and stored in the refrigerator, and then served directly to guests. It would be a hassle-free dish to serve in parties because it can be made ahead of time. You can have hot as well as cold dips and serve these with an array of chips and crudités, which can be made at home in various shapes and sizes according to the temperament of the calorie-conscious guests.

The book includes sections like hot and cold dips, fondues, quick dips, and chips. It has evergreen traditional favourites as well as innovative new ones and low-cal variations for the health conscious foodies. Recipes like **Green Mayonnaise, Asparagus Fondue, Achaari Dip, Chocolate Fondue,** and **Mango Salsa**, are sure to excite your gastronomic juices and stimulate you to go straight to the kitchen and put together some interesting chips and dips right away.

Tarla Dalal

CONTENTS

Fondues

Chips / Crudités

Basic Recipes

* This indicates sweet dips

DIPS

Thick, gooey dips that cling to the chips and refuse to let go... ah, the very image teases the taste buds. Dips add immense value to chips, crispy breads, and veggie finger foods. They add more colour, flavour and zing to the crispies. Chips and dips the made for each other couple together they make for great appetisers and are basically ideal for a snack any time during the day.

The phrase 'Chips and Dips' usually refers to some crunchy foodstuff to bite into, served along with a smooth or course dip into which the chips can be dipped. If the dip is smooth it can also be used as a spread on chips and breads. A chunky dip usually goes well with thick chips which can hold and lift the chunks with them. Dips can usually be whipped up quite fast and easily, as it is mostly just a matter of assembling and blending stuff. Dips could be served hot or cold depending on their ingredients.

Fondues are also an interesting variety of dips. The caveat is that they are usually served in special pots which have a candle or flame beneath, which simmers the dip while you enjoy it thick and hot. Special forks are used too. Firm chips that can easily be pierced and handled with a fork are usually used in combination with fondues. Fondues are ideal for summers and rainy weather.

Here we present a collection of interesting dips, including traditional favourites as well as innovative ones with unique combinations of ingredients.

9

HOT DIPS

❋ Curried Paneer Paté ❋

Picture on page 2.

Here's a smashing combination of paneer, celery and spring onions that adds josh to lavash and bread sticks.

Preparation time: 10 minutes.   Cooking time: 5 minutes.   Makes approx. 1 cup.

½ cup grated *paneer* (cottage cheese)
¼ cup chopped spring onion whites
2 tsp chopped celery
1 tsp curry powder
¼ tsp turmeric powder (*haldi*)
1 tbsp mayonnaise
2 tsp oil
¼ tsp pepper powder
Salt to taste

For serving
Lavash, page 90
Bread Sticks

1. Heat the oil in a pan, add the spring onion whites and celery and cook for 2 minutes till they turn soft.
2. Add the curry powder, turmeric powder and salt and mix well. Remove from flame and keep aside.
3. Combine the spring onion mixture, *paneer*, mayonnaise and pepper powder.
4. Mix while mashing continuously with the back of a spoon.
   Serve warm with lavash and bread sticks.

Handy Tip: To make the dip healthy use tofu instead of *paneer*.

✳ *Baked Beans Dip* ✳

Serve this very easy-to-make and tasty bean dip with tortilla chips. Beware, baked beans add such a sumptuous flavour to this dip, a whole bowl will be over before you know it.

Preparation time: 10 minutes.   Cooking time: 5 minutes.   Makes 2 cups.

1 can (450 grams) baked beans
3 tbsp grated cheese
4 tbsp tomato ketchup
½ tsp chilli powder
3 tsp chilli sauce
1 tsp oil
Salt to taste

For serving
¼ cup sour cream, page 101
Fat Free Wafers, page 96

1. Blend the beans to a smooth purée in a mixer.
2. Heat oil in a pan, add the beans purée along with the rest of the ingredients and let it cook for 2 to 3 minutes. If the mixture is too thick, add a little water.
3. In a bowl pour the dip and top with sour cream. Serve warm with fat free wafers.

✴ *Layered Pizza Dip* ✴

The taste buds tingle the moment you imagine layers of tomato sauce and sautéed capsicum topped with cheese and baked in the oven. Indulge in this extravaganza, with a bowlful of wafers.

Preparation time: 10 minutes.   Cooking time: 10 minutes.   Makes approx. 1 cup.
Baking temperature : 180°C (360°F).   Baking time : 15 to 20 minutes.

For the tomato sauce layer
2 tomatoes
¼ cup chopped onions
1 clove garlic
1 tsp oregano
1 tsp dried chilli flakes
1 tsp sugar
2 tsp oil
Salt to taste

For the capsicum layer
1 capsicum

1 tsp oil

Other ingredients
2 tbsp grated cheese

For serving
Fat Free Wafers, page 96
Vegetable Crudités, page 89

13

For the tomato sauce layer
1. Boil a vesselful of water, add the tomatoes and continue boiling for 2 to 3 minutes.
2. Remove and cool the tomatoes and allow them to cool.
3. Peel and chop them finely. Keep aside.
4. Heat the oil in a pan, add the onions and garlic and sauté till they are golden brown.
5. Add the tomatoes and cook for 5 to 7 minutes.
6. Add the oregano, chilli flakes, sugar and salt and cook for a couple of minutes. Keep aside.

For the capsicum layer
1. Cut the capsicum into thin slices.
2. Heat the oil in a pan, add the capsicum slices and sauté for a few minutes. Keep aside.

How to proceed
1. Take a glass bowl, layer the base with tomato sauce and then add a layer of the capsicum on it.
2. Top it with cheese.
3. Place the bowl in an oven at 180°C (360°F) for 5 minutes or till the cheese melts on top.
   Serve with fat free wafers and vegetable crudités.

❋ *Broccoli and Mushroom Dip* ❋

A generous helping of cheese adds a delectable texture to this creamy, saucy dip,
which is full of the flavour and goodness of broccoli and mushrooms.

Preparation time: 10 minutes.   Cooking time: 10 minutes.   Makes 2 cups.

1 cup broccoli florets
½ cup sliced mushrooms
¼ cup chopped onion
1 clove garlic, crushed
¼ tsp finely chopped green chillies
2 tbsp plain flour (*maida*)
1 cup milk
½ cup grated cheddar cheese
½ cup grated processed cheese
2 tbsp butter
Salt and pepper to taste

For serving
Pita Chips, page 97
Cream Crackers

1. Boil a vesselful of water. Add the broccoli and continue boiling for 2 minutes.
2. Drain and discard the water and put the broccoli in a vesselful of ice-cold water.
3. Drain after 5 minutes, discard the water and keep the broccoli aside.
4. Heat the butter in a pan and sauté the onions in it for 1 minute.
5. Add the garlic and green chillies and sauté again for a few seconds.
6. Add the flour and sauté for at least 1½ minutes on a slow flame.
7. Add the milk and cheese and cook till the mixture thickens.
8. Add the broccoli, mushrooms, salt and pepper and mix well.
   Serve warm with pita chips and cream crackers.

❋ *Indian Corn Dip* ❋

Picture on page 19.

*This is an interesting variation of the traditional corn dip. It has a creamy texture,
and is jazzed up with a unique combination of Indian spices.*

Preparation time: 5 minutes.   Cooking time: 5 minutes.   Makes 1 cup.

1 large sweet corn cob (*bhutta/makai*)
2 tsp cornflour
½ cup milk
½ tsp cumin seeds (*jeera*)
½ tsp mustard seeds (*rai / sarson*)
1 tbsp oil
Salt to taste

For garnish
Chopped coriander

For serving
Plain khakhras

1. Cut the sweet corn into 3 big pieces and boil them in a vesselful of water till tender.
2. Drain and discard the water.
3. Grate the corn cob and blend to a smooth purée in a mixer adding a little water Keep aside.
4. Heat oil in a non-stick pan and add the cumin seeds and mustard seeds.
5. When the seeds crackle add the prepared purée and salt and mix well. Cook for 2 minutes.
6. Mix the cornflour with milk, add to the purée and cook till the mixture thickens. Garnish with coriander and serve hot with plain khakhras.

INDIAN CORN DIP : Recipe on page 17. ↪

❊ *Herbed Tomato Dip* ❊

Liken this dip to pizza sauce if you will because it has got all the delightful Italian herbs, tangy tomatoes and molten cheese as well, but it tastes just too good with toasted triangles.

Preparation time: 10 minutes.   Cooking time: 10 minutes.   Makes approx 1½ cups.
Baking temperature : 150°C (300°F).   Baking time : 10 minutes.

2 tomatoes
¼ cup milk
¼ cup grated cheese
2 tbsp cream
1 tsp cornflour
1 tbsp mixed herbs
Salt to taste

For serving
Toasted triangles, page 88
Baked Tortilla Chips, page 98

1. Cut the tomatoes into thick slices. Place them on a greased baking tray and sprinkle the herbs and salt over them.
2. Bake in a pre-heated oven for 5 minutes at 150°C (300°F) or microwave on HIGH for 2 minutes.
3. Remove, peel and roughly chop the tomatoes. Keep aside.
4. Heat the milk, cheese and cream in a pan till the cheese melts.
5. Mix the cornflour with 3 tbsp water and add it to the pan. Cook till the mixture thickens.
6. Remove the sauce from flame and mix in the tomatoes.
   Serve hot with toasted bread and breadsticks.

Handy Tip: The dip is supposed to taste a bit sour but you could add a pinch of sugar in it if you like.

✳ *Layered Mexican Dip* ✳

Picture on page 75.

Sally forth to Mexico! Rajma (kidney beans) cooked with the famous salsa sauce and topped with cheese, transforms into a delectable layered dip, which tastes fabulous with corn chips.

Preparation time: 10 minutes.   Cooking time: 30 minutes.   Makes 1½ cups.
Baking temperature : 180°C (360°F).   Baking time : 5 minutes.

For the salsa sauce
1 tomato
1 tbsp finely chopped onion
¼ tsp chilli powder
¼ tsp oregano
½ tsp sugar
½ tsp salt
2 tsp oil

For the refried beans
¼ cup red *rajma* (kidney beans)
¼ cup chopped tomatoes

1 small clove garlic, crushed
1 tsp finely chopped green chillies
½ cup chopped onions
½ tsp chilli powder
½ tsp roasted cumin seeds (*jeera*) powder
½ tsp sugar
½ tbsp oil
Salt to taste

Other ingredients
¼ cup grated cheese

For serving
Baked Tortilla Chips, page 98

For the salsa sauce
1. Put the tomato in hot water for about 1 minute. Remove the skin and chop.
2. Heat the oil and fry the onion for ½ minute. Add the remaining ingredients and cook for 2 minutes.

For the refried beans

1. Wash the *rajma* and soak in water overnight. Next day, drain.
2. Add the tomatoes, garlic, green chillies and half the onions and put to cook in a pressure cooker. Drain. Keep aside the drained water.
3. Heat the oil and fry the remaining onions for ½ minute.
4. Add the *rajma*, chilli powder, cumin seeds powder, sugar, butter and salt and cook for 2 to 3 minutes.
5. Mash the *rajma* coarsely. If the mixture is dry, add the drained water.

How to proceed

1. Layer a transparent glass bowl with refried beans, on top of that the salsa sauce and the grated cheese.
2. Bake in an oven at 180°C (360°F) till the cheese melts.
   Serve hot with baked tortilla chips.

❋ *Mocha Dip* ❋

Like a mocha cappuccino with a sprinkling of cinnamon on top, this dip proves to be a perfect end to a party fare. Dip a piece of vanilla sponge cake into mocha dip, pop into your mouth, sit back and enjoy as it melts its way into your heart.

Preparation time: 5 minutes.   Cooking time: 2 minutes.   Makes approx. ¾ cup.

½ cup grated dark chocolate
½ cup fresh cream
1 tsp coffee powder

For serving
Vanilla sponge cake, cut into pieces
Marshmallows

1. Mix the coffee powder with 2 tsp water and heat for a minute. Keep aside.
2. Combine chocolate and cream and heat on a low flame so it melts.
3. Add the coffee mixture, mix well and serve at room temperature with vanilla sponge and marshmallows.

Handy tip : The dip is supposed to taste bitter. But if you want to make a sweet dip, use plain chocolate but remember the colour will not be so dark.

✳ *Corn Dip* ✳

This sweet and sour sweet-corn dip, when served with toasted triangles or some wafers, is a delectable treat that can be enjoyed at any time of the day.

Preparation time: 5 minutes.   Cooking time: 5 minutes.   Makes approx. 1½ cups.

1 large sweet corn (*bhutta / makai*)
2 tsp cornflour
½ cup milk
¼ cup grated cheese
½ tsp mustard sauce
Few drops of Tabasco sauce
Salt to taste
Freshly ground pepper to taste

For serving
Toasted Triangles, page 88
Potato Wedges, page 92

1. Dissolve the cornflour in the milk and keep aside.
2. Cut the sweet corn into 3 big pieces and boil them in a vessel full of water till done.
3. Drain and discard the water.
4. Grate the corn cob and blend the grated corn to a smooth purée in a mixer using a little water.
5. Heat a non-stick pan, add the purée and sauté for a couple of minutes.
6. Add the cornflour-milk mixture to the purée and cook till the mixture thickens.
7. Add the cheese, mustard sauce, salt and pepper. Mix well and switch off the flame.
8. Add the Tabasco sauce and serve immediately with toasted triangles and potato wedges.

COLD DIPS

✴ *Spinach and Tofu Dip* ✴

Picture on page 1.

*Here is an interesting variation of the staid spinach dip, which tastes great with pita chips.
The infusion of tofu into this creamy-textured dip makes it a light and a healthy option.*

Preparation time: 5 minutes.   Cooking time: 5 minutes.   Makes approx 1 cup.

3 cups washed and shredded spinach (*palak*)
¾ cup roughly chopped *tofu* (soya *paneer*)
¼ cup sliced onions
1 tsp lemon juice
1 tsp oregano
2 tbsp oil
Salt and freshly ground pepper to taste

For serving
Pita Chips, page 97
Toasted Triangles, page 88

28

1. In a pan add the spinach and cook on a high flame for a minute to remove its moisture. Remove from the pan and keep aside.
2. Heat 1 tbsp of oil in the same pan, add the onions and sauté till they turn translucent.
3. Combine the onions, spinach, tofu, lemon juice, oregano, remaining 1 tbsp of oil, salt and pepper and blend in a mixer to make a thick paste.
4. Keep refrigerated for at least an hour. Served chilled with pita chips and toasted triangles.

✳ *3-Layered Cold Dip* ✳

This attractive and innovative dip comprises three sauces layered one above the other in a bowl: pesto sauce loaded with basil, the famous Italian herb; milky cream cheese sauce with a dash of herbs; and sun-dried tomato sauce.

Preparation time: 10 minutes.   Cooking time: Nil.   Makes 1½ cups.

½ cup cream cheese, page 100
½ cup sundried tomatoes, page 102

For the pesto layer
¼ cup chopped pine nuts *(chilgoza)* or walnuts
2 cups fresh basil leaves, loosely packed
2 tbsp olive oil
1 tsp chopped garlic
Salt to taste

For serving
Vegetable Crudités, page 89
Potato Fries

For the pesto layer
1. Lightly roast the pine nuts. Cool completely.
2. Combine all the ingredients in a mixer and blend into a smooth paste. Keep aside.

How to proceed
1. Soak the sun-dried tomatoes in a little warm water for about 5 minutes and blend to a fine paste.
2. Put the cream cheese, pesto and sun-dried tomato paste in different layers in a bowl.
3. Keep refrigerated for at least an hour. Served chilled with hot potato fries or vegetable crudités.

✴ *Achaari Dip* ✴

Picture on page 85.

Never before would you have seen such a variety of Indian spices assemble together to create a lip-smacking Achaari dip. Enjoy!

Preparation time: A few minutes.   Cooking time: 2 minutes.   Makes 1 cup.

¾ cup chilled hung curds (*dahi*), whisked
¼ cup chopped coriander
½ tsp finely chopped green chillies
Salt to taste
Sugar to taste

For the achaari spices
¼ tsp fenugreek (*methi*) seeds
¼ tsp mustard seeds (*rai / sarson*)
½ tsp cumin seeds (*jeera*)
½ tsp fennel seeds (*saunf*)
¼ tsp onion seeds (*kalongi*)
A pinch of asafoetida (*hing*)
½ tsp oil

32

For serving
Plain Khakhras

For the achaari spices
1. Heat the oil in a pan, add the fenugreek seeds, mustard seeds, cumin seeds, fennel seeds and onion seeds.
2. When the seeds crackle add the asafoetida and switch off the gas.
3. Remove and keep aside.

How to proceed
1. Combine the achaari spices, coriander, green chillies, salt and sugar together in a mixer and blend to a fine paste using little water.
2. Pour it into a bowl, add the curds and whisk well. Serve immediately with khakhras.

❋ *Authentic Hummus* ❋

Hummus, the famous traditional Lebanese spread, has a creamy chickpea texture. It tastes fantastic when served as apart of a mezze platter with flat breads or vegetables.

Preparation time: 20 minutes.   Cooking time: 15 minutes.   Makes 1 cup.

¼ cup *kabuli chana* (chick peas)
2 cloves garlic
4 tbsp fresh curds (*dahi*)
Juice of 1 lemon
3 tbsp olive oil
Salt to taste

For the garnish
Chopped parsley
Chilli powder
1 tsp olive oil

For serving
Lavash, page 90

1. Soak the *kabuli chana* in water for 6 hours. Drain, wash, add ¾ cup of water and salt and pressure cook till the *chana* is done. Cool, drain and keep the water aside.
2. Combine the *kabuli chana* with the garlic, curds, lemon juice, olive oil, salt and a little strained water in a mixer and blend to a smooth paste. If the mixture is too thick, add a little more of the water.
3. Place this mixture in a serving plate and sprinkle parsley and chilli powder and olive oil on top.
   Serve with Lavash.

Variation : **Herbed Hummus**
    Just add 2 tsp of mixed dried herbs at step 2 in the above recipe.

✳ *Walnut Vegetable Paté* ✳

Picture on facing page.

The walnut vegetable pate serves as an interesting appetiser. Subtle flavour of garlic mingled with walnuts and vegetables to make a delectable paté.

Preparation time: 10 minutes.   Cooking time: 2 minutes.
Makes approx 1 cup.

¼ cup walnuts (*akhrot*)
1 cup finely chopped mixed vegetables (mushrooms, spring onions, carrots, capsicum)
1 tsp chopped garlic
½ tsp mixed dried herbs
2 tsp olive oil
Salt to taste

For serving
Toasted Triangles, page 88
Tabasco sauce
Few torn lettuce leaves
Cherry tomatoes, halved

WALNUT VEGETABLE PATÉ : Recipe above. ↦

1. Heat the oil in a pan, add all the vegetables and sauté for 2 minutes. Remove and keep aside.
2. Combine the walnuts, sautéed vegetables, garlic, mixed dried herbs and salt together and blend in a mixer with a little water to a grainy purée.

For serving
Place a small piece of lettuce on toasted triangles. Spoon out little paté on the leaves and top with few drops of Tabasco sauce.
Garnish with half of cherry tomato and serve immediately.

✴ *Black Bean Dip* ✴

Healthy and yummy black beans belong to the high-fibre legume family. This dip can be stored in the fridge for up to a week! This is not really a creamy dip, but more like a salad to munch on with some chips.

Preparation time: 10 minutes.   Cooking time: 20 minutes.   Makes 1 cup.

¼ cup black beans
¼ cup finely chopped onions
¼ cup finely chopped tomatoes
1 tsp lemon juice
½ tsp roasted cumin seeds (*jeera*) powder
Salt to taste

For serving
Pita Chips, page 97

1. Pressure cook black beans with 1½ cups of water and salt for 2 whistles or till they are done.
2. Cool, drain and discard the water.
3. Combine all the remaining ingredients with the black beans in a bowl.
4. Lightly mash with the back of a spoon.
   Serve with pita chips.

✳ *Babaganoush* ✳

The smoky aroma and taste of grilled eggplant gives this traditional Greek dish a distinctive flavour, just as garlic adds a sharp tinge to it. It can be served with pita as part of a mezze platter.

Preparation time: 15 minutes.   Cooking time: 15 minutes.   Makes 1½ cups.

1 large (250 grams) brinjal (*baingan* / eggplant)
2 large cloves garlic
¼ cup thick curds (*dahi*)
1 tsp chopped green chilli
¼ tsp cumin seeds (*jeera*) powder
2 spring onions, finely chopped
1 tbsp chopped coriander
Salt to taste

Other ingredients
Oil for greasing

For serving
Pita Chips, page 97

1. Prick the brinjals with a fork, grease with oil and place over a grill or gas flame. Rotate it regularly till the peel is almost burnt and the flesh is soft and pulpy. Allow it to cool.
2. Carefully peel the burnt skin and discard it.
3. Put the brinjal pulp in a blender, add the garlic, curds and green chilli and blend in a mixer to a smooth purée.
4. Transfer to a bowl, add the cumin powder, spring onions, coriander and salt and mix well.
5. Keep refrigerated for at least an hour. Served chilled with pita chips.

✳ *Garlicky Lentil Purée* ✳

Quick-to-cook tender red lentils absorb the deep garlic flavour in this dip, which is pepped up with a dose of lemon juice, a subtle infusion of cumin, and a blast of chilli powder. For a through-and-through garlic fest, serve this dip with bread sticks.

Preparation time: 5 minutes.   Cooking time: 10 minutes.   Makes approx. 1 cup.

½ cup whole *masoor* (whole red lentils)
3 cloves of garlic
1 tsp lemon juice
1 tsp roasted cumin seeds (*jeera*)
¼ tsp red chilli powder
2 tsp olive oil
Salt to taste

For serving
Bread sticks

1. Wash the *masoor* and pressure cook with 1½ cups of water for 3 whistles. Remove and keep aside. Do not drain the water.
2. Roast the garlic cloves on open flame (low) till they are brown but not burnt.
3. Combine all the ingredients including the *masoor* and garlic in a mixer and blend to a smooth purée.
   Serve warm with bread sticks.

❋ *Labneh* ❋

Labneh is a popular mezze dish, and serves as an interesting alternative to sour cream or cream cheese. Made from hung curds and seasoned with garlic, the pungent dip tastes great when spread on bread, bagels, or fresh pita. It has a prominent presence on the breakfast table, in Middle Eastern households.

Preparation time: 20 minutes.   Cooking time: 5 minutes.   Makes 1 cup.

1 cup thick hung curds (*dahi*)
1 tbsp fresh cream
2 cloves garlic, grated
2 tsp roasted sesame seeds (*til*)
1 tbsp olive oil
Salt to taste

For serving
Vegetable Crudités, page 89
Pita Chips, page 97

1. Pound the sesame seeds and olive oil in a mortar and pestle to form a smooth paste.
2. Put in a bowl, add all the remaining ingredients and whisk well.
3. Keep refrigerated for at least an hour. Served chilled with vegetable crudités and pita chips.

✦ Tahini Dip ✦

Picture on back cover.

A traditional Middle Eastern dip made of roasted lentils and seeds mixed with hung curds.
This creamy dip is nutrient-rich too, and includes a generous dose of proteins and iron.

Preparation time: 10 minutes. Cooking time: 20 minutes. Makes approx. 1 cup.

¼ cup sesame seeds *(til)*
2 tbsp *chana dal* (split Bengal gram)
2 tbsp fresh curds *(dahi)*
½ tsp vinegar
1 tsp finely chopped garlic
1 tsp green chillies
½ tsp chilli powder
½ tsp cumin seeds *(jeera)* powder
½ tsp oil
Salt to taste

For serving
Lavash, page 90

1. Dry roast the sesame seeds and *chana dal* separately. Grind them together in a mixer to a fine powder. Keep aside.
2. Whisk together the curds, vinegar, garlic, green chillies, oil and salt in a bowl.
3. Add the roasted powder and mix well.
4. Sprinkle chilli powder, and cumin seed powder on top of the mixture.
5. Keep refrigerated for atleast an hour. Served chilled with lavash.

✦ *Muhhamarra* ✦

Muhhamarra is a spicy dip of Middle-Eastern origin. Made by coarsely grinding red pepper with nuts, this easy-to-make dip can be served warm or cold.

Preparation time: 15 minutes.   Cooking time: Nil.   Makes approx. 1 cup.

¾ cup chopped walnuts (*akhrot*)
2 whole dry Kashmiri red chillies
2 tsp chopped garlic
½ cup fresh bread crumbs, refer handy tip
1 tbsp pomegranate seeds (*anardana*)
¼ cup olive oil
Salt to taste

For serving
Lavash, page 90
Pita Chips, page 97

1. Soak the dry red chillies in warm water for about 15 minutes. Drain and discard the water.
2. Combine all the ingredients including the red chillies and blend to a smooth paste with ¼ cup of water.

   Serve with lavash and pita chips.

Handy tip : To make fresh bread crumbs, just blend fresh bread in a mixer.

✳ *Herb Cheese Slices on Crackers* ✳

Dip into this herb-flavoured spread made by combining cottage cheese with yoghurt, parsley and dill, to beat the summer heat.

Preparation time: 5 minutes.   Cooking time: Nil.   Makes 8 slices.

¾ cup grated *paneer* (cottage cheese)
1 tbsp fresh curds (*dahi*)
1 tbsp chopped parsley
½ tsp chopped dill (*suva bhaji*)
1 clove garlic, grated
1 green chilli, chopped
Salt to taste

For serving
Cream Crackers

1. Combine all the ingredients in a mixer and blend till smooth.
2. Spread over plastic film and roll into a cylinder of 37 mm. (1½") diameter.

3. Refrigerate till firm.
4. Unwrap the plastic film and cut into thick slices.

For serving
Place a thick slice of herb cheese on a cream cracker and serve immediately.

❋ *Chunky Asparagus Delight* ❋

Picture on page 55.

Whirled to a delicate smoothness and lightness, this mixture is heartily loaded with asparagus and an interesting flavouring of agar agar, sour cream and Tabasco sauce.

Preparation time: 10 minutes.   Cooking time: 25 minutes.   Makes 8 pieces.

For Asparagus Mousse
½ cup asparagus, cut into ¼" long pieces
2 cups vegetable stock
5 gms *agar agar* (unflavoured china grass)
Salt to taste

For serving
Sour Cream, page 101
Cream Crackers
Tabasco or Capsico sauce

1. Boil the asparagus in water till they become tender. Keep aside.
2. Mix the vegetable stock and *agar agar* and boil till the *agar agar* melts.
3. Strain the liquid and add salt. Mix gently.
4. Arrange the asparagus stem in a 3" x 5" baking dish and pour the *agar agar* mixture on top of it.
5. Once the mixture is set cut into squares.
6. Refrigerate for at least an hour. Remove and cut into 8 bite sized pieces.

For serving
Place one asparagus mousse piece on a cream cracker, top with some sour cream. Serve immediately along with Tabasco or Capsico Sauce.

Handy tip : To make vegetable stock, just add vegetables like carrots, spring onions, capsicum and white pumpkin to a vesselful of water and simmer for about 20 minutes. Strain, use the liquid as stock and discard the vegetables.

CHUNKY ASPARAGUS DELIGHT : Recipe on page 53. →

✳ *Spinach Dip* ✳

Spinach and walnuts come together with nutmeg and garlic in this rich dip, which tastes excellent with cheesy bread strips.

Preparation time: 10 minutes.   Cooking time: 10 minutes.   Makes 1 cup.

½ cup chopped spinach (*palak*)
½ cup walnuts (*akhrot*)
1 tsp finely chopped garlic
½ cup fresh curds (*dahi*)
2 tsp green chillies
½ tsp nutmeg (*jaiphal*)
Salt to taste

For serving
Cheesy Bread Strips, page 95

1. Wash the chopped spinach and steam for 1 minute. Cool and squeeze to remove all the water. Keep aside.
2. Combine the walnuts and garlic and blend to a smooth paste in mixer.
3. Add the oil and spinach alternatively and keep blending till the mixture is smooth and thick.
4. Add the salt, nutmeg and curds to make a mixture of dipping consistency.
5. Keep refrigerated for at least an hour. Served chilled with Cheesy Bread Strips.

✴ *Avocado Dip* ✴

Looking to spice up the tortilla chips? Why not whip up this wonderful yet easy-to-make guacamole dip. Top with tomatoes and lace with lemon juice, and enjoy the surprisingly pleasant sourness.

Preparation time: 10 minutes.   Cooking time: Nil.   Makes 1 cup.

2 ripe avocados
2 tbsp finely chopped onion whites
1½ tbsp lemon juice
1 tbsp chopped tomatoes
1 tsp chopped green chillies
Salt to taste

For serving
Jeera Kand Wafers, page 94
Potato Wedges, page 92

1. Cut the avocados into half and scoop out all the pulp. Mash it with the back of a spoon.
2. Add all the remaining ingredients and mix well.
3. Keep refrigerated for at least an hour. Served chilled.
   Serve with baked tortilla chips and potato wedges.

Handy tip : Put a little lemon juice in a thin layer on the surface of the avocado dip. Keep covered to prevent it from oxidising and turning black.

✽ *Roasted Bell Pepper Dip* ✽

This dip has an unbeatable aroma and flavour, thanks to the exotic flavour of roasted bell peppers.
Serve hot along with potato wedges.

Preparation time: 5 minutes.   Cooking time: 20 minutes.   Makes approx. 1 cup.

2 red bell peppers (capsicum)
¼ cup mayonnaise
¼ tsp dry red chilli flakes
Salt to taste
Oil for greasing

For serving
Potato Wedges, page 92

1. Wash the bell peppers, grease them lightly and pierce forks through each one
2. Roast them on a open high flame till they soften and the skin is charred.
3. Wash them in cold water and remove the burnt skin. Chop roughly.
4. Blend the mayonnaise, paprika, roasted bell peppers and salt in a mixer to make a smooth paste.
   Serve warm along with potato wedges.

❈ *Quick Asparagus Mousse* ❈

Dip into this delightfully cold, refreshing blend of asparagus and cheese, pepped up with a sprinkling of salt and pepper.

Preparation time: 5 minutes.   Cooking time: Nil.   Makes 1½ cups.

1 can (400 gm) asparagus
3 tbsp grated cheese
½ cup fresh cream
Salt and pepper to taste

For serving
Bread Sticks

1. Drain the water from the tin and chop the asparagus.
2. Blend together the asparagus, cheese, cream, salt and pepper.
3. Transfer the mixture to a serving bowl and refrigerate till set.
   Serve with bread sticks.

✴ *Citrus Salsa with Spicy Coriander* ✴

Time to tango with tangy oranges! This green and orange salsa not only looks good but also tastes good, and is healthy as well.

Preparation time: 10 minutes.   Cooking time: Nil.   Makes approx. 1 cup.

½ cup chopped oranges
½ cup chopped sweet lime (*mosambi*)
¼ cup chopped tomatoes
¼ cup chopped coriander
1 tsp roasted cumin seed (*jeera*) powder
½ tsp chilli powder
Salt to taste

For serving
Baked Tortilla Chips, page 98

Mix all the ingredients in a bowl and let them marinate for atleast one hour in the refrigerator.
Serve chilled with baked tortilla chips.

✳ *Mango Salsa* ✳

Picture on page 65.

This colourful, delicious and easy-to-make dish combines fresh coriander leaves with the tantalizing flavour of mango to create a unique salsa.

Preparation time: 10 minutes.   Cooking time: Nil.   Makes approx. 1¼ cups.

½ cup chopped ripe mangoes
½ cup chopped tomatoes
1 tbsp chopped celery
2 tbsp chopped spring onion whites
1 tbsp chopped capsicum
½ tsp dry red chilli flakes
Salt to taste

For serving
Tortilla Chips

1. Mix the mangoes and tomatoes in a bowl and lightly mash them with the back of a spoon.

2. Add the remaining ingredients, mix well and let them marinate for atleast one
   hour in the refrigerator.
   Serve chilled with baked tortilla chips.

Handy tip: Add a few drops of lemon juice if the salsa is too sweet.

Variation: Peach Salsa

Substitute ½ cup of chopped mangoes with ½ cup of chopped fresh
peaches.

MANGO SALSA : Recipe on page 63. →

✳ *Walnut Dip* ✳

This nutty dip, made with ground walnuts and curds, adds crackle and sparkle to pita chips and cream crackers.

Preparation time: 10 minutes.   Cooking time: Nil.   Makes 1 cup.

3 tbsp walnuts *(akhrot)*
½ cup *paneer* (cottage cheese)
3 tsp milk
3 tbsp curds *(dahi)*
1 tsp parsley
Salt to taste

For serving
Vegetable Crudités, page 89
Cream crackers

1. Grind the walnuts coarsely in a blender.
2. Combine the walnuts; *paneer,* milk, curds and parsley and blend in a mixer till it becomes a smooth paste.
3. Mix in the walnuts and keep refrigerated for at least an hour.
   Served chilled with pita chips and cream crackers.

❋ *Veg Cream Cheese Dip* ❋

A flavourful, cool, fresh-tasting dip that goes well with vegetables and crackers. Just add a dash of cream cheese, sour cream and chilli, and there you have all the zing needed to lift you beyond mundane everyday worries.

Preparation time: 5 minutes.   Cooking time: Nil.   Makes approx. 1 cup.

½ cup grated *paneer* (cottage cheese)
¼ cup fresh hung curds (*dahi*)
2 tbsp grated radish
2 tbsp grated carrots
1 tbsp finely chopped celery
Dry red chilli flakes to taste
Salt to taste

For serving
Pita Chips, page 97
Jeera Kand Wafers, page 94

1. Blend the *paneer* and curds in a mixer to a smooth paste.
2. Pour into a bowl, add the remaining ingredients and mix well.
   Serve with pita chips and jeera kand wafers.

✴ *Spiced Tandoori Dip* ✴

Try this combination of tomatoes and thick curds, steeped in the fascinating flavour of Tandoori masala, to add zing to vegetable crudités.

Preparation time: 5 minutes.   Cooking time: Nil.   Makes 1 cup.

¾ cup fresh thick curds (*dahi*)
½ cup chopped tomatoes
¼ cup chopped coriander
1 tbsp *tandoori masala*
A pinch of sugar
Salt to taste

For serving
Vegetable Crudités, page 89

Combine all the ingredients in a mixer and blend to a smooth thick paste.
Serve with vegetable crudités.

Handy tip : For a smoother dip, deseed the tomatoes but retain the pulp.

✳ *Green Mayonnaise* ✳

No other mayonnaise dip can compete with this fascinating combination of mayonnaise, parsley, and coriander, spiked with onions and green chillies. Tastes great with homemade toasted triangle.

Preparation time: 5 minutes.   Cooking time: 10 minutes.   Makes 1¼ cup.

1 cup mayonnaise
½ cup chopped coriander
¼ cup chopped parsley
2 tsp green chillies
1 tbsp finely chopped onions
4 to 5 drops lemon juice

For serving
Toasted Triangles, page 88
Potato Fries

1. Combine the coriander, parsley, green chillies, onions and lemon juice in a mixer and blend to a smooth paste.
2. Pour into a bowl, add the mayonnaise and mix well.
3. Keep refrigerated for at least an hour.
   Served chilled with toasted triangles and potato fries.

FONDUES

✴ *Cheese Fondue* ✴

Coat your homemade toasted triangles with this creamy gooey garlic-flavoured fondue, for an unforgettable experience. Don't forget to add the white wine!

Preparation time: 10 minutes.   Cooking time: 10 minutes.   Makes 1 cup.

100 grams grated cooking cheese (use combination of two strong cheeses)
1 clove crushed garlic
1 tbsp plain flour (*maida*)
1 cup milk
1 tbsp white wine
1 tbsp butter
Salt and freshly ground pepper to taste

For serving
Vegetable Crudités, page 89
Lavash, page 90

1. Heat the butter in a saucepan, add the garlic and sauté for ½ a minute.
2. Add the flour and fry for another minute.
3. Add the milk and go on stirring and cooking until the mixture becomes thick and no lumps remain.
4. Reduce the flame, add the white wine and cheese gradually and go on stirring till the mixture becomes a smooth sauce of coating consistency.
5. Finally, add very little salt and pepper.
   Serve hot with vegetable crudités and lavash.

✳ *Classic Chocolate Fondue* ✳

Divinely rich and silky smooth, chocolate fondue doesn't get much better unless you add the rich creamy chocolate and brandy. To melt in your mouth served with the chewy marsh mellows and cut fruits.

Preparation time: 10 minutes.   Cooking time: 5 minutes.   Makes 1 cup.

½ cup plain or milk chocolate, broken into small pieces
1 tbsp plain flour (*maida*)
½ cup milk
3 tbsp cocoa powder
1 cup beaten cream
4 to 5 tbsp sugar
½ tsp vanilla essence
1 tbsp butter
2 tbsp brandy (optional)

For Serving
Stewed or fresh fruit, marshmallows, cake pieces

1. Heat the butter in a pan, add the flour and cook for 2 minutes till you get the aroma of cooked flour.
2. Add the milk, chocolate pieces, cocoa powder, cream, sugar and ¾ cup of water and cook stirring continuously till the mixture thickens.
3. Put the mixture in a fondue pot, stir in vanilla essence and brandy.
   Serve with stewed or fresh fruit, marshmallows, cake pieces.

LAYERED MEXICAN DIP : Recipe on page 22. →

Roasted Tomato and Capsicum Fondue

Picture on cover.

The delectable flavour of flame-roasted tomato and capsicum makes this a unique dip, which all your guests are sure to woo. Serve this with toasted croutons and be prepared to take a million calls from your guests the day after the party, asking for the recipe!

Preparation time: 10 minutes.   Cooking time: 10 minutes.   Makes approx. 1 cup.

1 tomato
½ red capsicum
3 tbsp finely chopped onions
½ tsp finely chopped garlic
½ cup grated cheese
1 tsp cornflour
2 tbsp milk
3 tsp butter
Salt to taste
Oil for greasing

For serving
Toasted Trangles, page 88
Vegetable Crudités, page 89

1. Pierce the tomato and red capsicum with forks, grease them lightly and roast separately on an open flame (low) till their skin turns black.
2. Peel, wash thoroughly, chop roughly and blend to a fine purée. Keep aside.
3. Heat the butter in a pan, add the onions and garlic and sauté till the onions turn translucent.
4. Add the prepared purée, cheese and salt and cook for a few minutes.
5. Mix the cornflour with milk and add it to the pan. Cook till the mixture thickens. Serve hot with toasted croutons.

✴ *Spinach Fondue* ✴

Never would you have imagined that spinach can taste so good. This thick, cheese-loaded spinach fondue is a perfect combo for toasted croutons.

Preparation time: 10 minutes.   Cooking time: 15 minutes.   Makes 1 cup.

1½ cup chopped spinach (*palak*)
¼ cup white wine (optional) or water
1 cup fresh cream
½ cup cheese
2 tbsp cornflour dissolved In ¼ cup of water
Salt and pepper to taste

For serving
Cheesy Bread Strips, page 95

1. Steam the spinach leaves. Squeeze out the water and blend the in a mixer to a smooth purée.
2. Pour into a saucepan, add all the remaining ingredients and cook on a low flame while stirring continuously till the mixture becomes thick.
3. Add salt and pepper, mix well and pour into a fondue pot.
   Serve with cheesy bread strips.

✴ *Asparagus Fondue* ✴

This rich, thick, creamy fondue made with asparagus and a generous portion of cheese, goes well with potato wedges and pita chips.

Preparation time: 10 minutes.   Cooking time: 15 minutes.   Makes 1 cup.

5 asparagus sticks
1 tsp butter
2 tbsp milk
½ cup grated cheese
1 tsp cornflour dissolved 1 tsp water
2 tbsp cream
Salt and pepper to taste

For serving
Potato Wedges, page 92
Pita Chips, page 97

1. Cut the asparagus spears (tips) and keep aside.
2. Boil 1 cup of water add the asparagus and cook till it softens.

3. Remove from flame, cool and puree. Strain the purée through a sieve to get a smooth paste
4. Heat the butter in a pan add the asparagus spears (tips), and sauté till they are cooked.
5. Add the milk, cheese, cornflour mixer stir till the cheese melts and till the mixture thickens.
6. Mix the asparagus puree, salt and pepper and cook for 5 minutes.
7. Switch off the flame stir in cream and serve hot in a fondue pot with potato wedges and pita chips.

✳ *Spicy Corn and Jalapeno Fondue* ✳

Your guests are all going to be buzzing around your fondue pot! Jalapenos favour the otherwise simple combination of corn, onions, capsicums and tomatoes, with an exotic flavour.

Preparation time: 10 minutes.   Cooking time: 10 minutes.   Makes 1 cup.

¼ cup boiled corn
1 tbsp chopped onion
2 tbsp chopped capsicum (red, yellow, green)
2 tbsp deseeded tomatoes
1 clove garlic, finely chopped
¼ cup milk
½ cup grated cheese
1 tsp cornflour dissolved in 1 tsp water
1½ tsp sliced jalapenos
1 tsp cream
1 tbsp olive oil
Salt to taste

For serving
Baked Tortilla Chips, page 98
Lavash, page 90

1. Heat the oil in a pan, add onions and sauté for 1 minute.
2. Add garlic, capsicum and tomatoes and sauté for 2 more minutes.
3. Add the corn to the vegetables, and cook on low flame for another 1 minute.
4. Add the milk, cheese, cornflour mixture stir till the cheese melts and the mixture thickens.
5. Add the jalapenos and salt and cook for 2 minutes.
6. Switch off the flame, stir in cream and serve hot in a fondue pot with tortilla chips and lavash.

✴ *Coconut Fondue* ✴

The subtle and elegant flavour of coconut milk gets a funky facelift thanks to the addition of orange juice. Delight in a combo of coconut fondue with pineapple and banana cubes.

Preparation time: 5 minutes.   Cooking time: 10 minutes.   Makes approx. 1 cup.

1 cup coconut milk
½ cup orange juice
½ tbsp lemon juice
6 tbsp sugar
2 tsp cornflour
A few drops of coconut essence

For serving
Pineapple and banana cubes

1. Dissolve the cornflour in the coconut milk and pour into a pan.
2. Add the remaining ingredients and cook for 5 minutes while stirring continuously till the mixture thickens.
3. Cool and refrigerate to chill.
   Serve chilled with pineapple and banana cubes.

ACHAARI DIP: Recipe on page 32. →

CHIPS

Crunchy munchy chips, breads, savouries and colourful veggie dippers of all types and sizes, with yummy crudités to add to this fun. My, who can stay away from a veritable spread of crunchies when served with an equally tantalising choice of dips to dig into! Hot from the oven, crisp from the frying pan, the world of chips is certainly an interesting one. No wonder then that baskets full of crispies vanish even before you know it.

This book will give you a good insight into a variety of chips that can be made at home, and help you make the perfect chip, with the right colour, texture and flavour, guaranteed to please your taste buds. There are variations to each chip, as you can make them more interesting with mixed herbs, Indian spices as well as pureed vegetables that really pep up the chips and make them even more interesting.

For example the famous Indian bread **naan,** which can either be baked or fried, can be mixed with some Indian spices or herbs that add more zing to it. It can be served as a chip along with an Indian dip to enhance its taste. **Dhokla, khakhras,** and **masala puri** are the Indian versions of chips, which can be eaten with various savoury dips. There is an endless list of international chips as well. For example, **potato wedges** can be made in different shapes to make them more tantalising, and **doughnuts** can be dipped in sweet dips or **fondue** to delight the sweet tooth. **Onion rings, crackers, pretzels, cheese swirls...** the list of crunchies and the dips that complement them is quite long and exciting.

Chips can be made easily at home. Once you have the basic ingredients you can easily make the chips, and if you tap into your imagination, you can serve them in innovative *avatars* pepped up with various herbs and spices. Here are couple of recipes that you can make at home without worrying about where to procure fancy, exotic ingredients from.

CHIPS / CRUDITÉS

✴ *Toasted Triangles* ✴

Next time you think bread is boring, try making these crispy toasted triangles, with the magical touch of olive oil and garlic.

Preparation time: 5 minutes.   Cooking time: Nil.   Makes 16 triangles.
Baking temperature : 150°C (300°F).   Baking time : 10 minutes.

4 bread slices
2 cloves garlic, lightly crushed
1 tbsp olive oil
Salt to taste

1. Cut each bread slice into 4 small triangles.
2. Apply olive oil evenly on the triangles and bake in a pre-heated oven at 150°C (300°F) for 2 minutes.
3. Remove and rub the crushed garlic on the triangles and sprinkle salt. Bake again at 150°C (300°F) for 5 minutes or till the bread is toasted well.

✳ *Vegetable Crudités* ✳

Picture on cover.

A healthy and nutrient-rich veggie platter that makes a perfect starter when served with an appropriate dip or fondue.

Preparation time: 5 minutes.   Cooking time: 30 minutes.   Serves 4.

½ cup carrot, cut into 1½" long strips
½ cup cucumber, cut into 1½" long strips
½ cup broccoli, cut into 1½" long strips
½ cup cauliflower, cut into 1½" long strips
Salt and pepper to taste

1. Fill a pot with ¾ full of water. Bring to boil and add salt.
2. Add the broccoli and cauliflower in the boiling water and boil for about 1 minute.
3. Strain the boiled vegetables in a colander.
4. Put the boiled vegetables in cold water and drain in a colander.
   Serve the carrot sticks and cucumber sticks raw.

❋ *Lavash* ❋

Picture on back cover.

Lavash, also known as Armenian cracker bread, is a deliciously soft bread made with maida, and topped with roasted sesame seeds and poppy seeds.

Preparation time: 10 minutes.   Cooking time: 45 minutes.   Makes approx. 25 chips.
Baking temperature : 180°C (360°F).   Baking time : 15 minutes.

¾ cup plain flour (*maida*)
½ tsp dry yeast
A pinch sugar
4 tbsp roasted sesame seeds (*til*)
3 tbsp poppy seeds (*khus-khus*)
2½ tbsp olive oil or oil
Salt to taste

1. Combine the yeast and sugar with ½ cup of warm water in a bowl. Cover and keep aside till it becomes frothy. (Approx. 10 minutes.)
2. Sift the flour. Make a well in the centre and add the yeast and sugar mixture and enough water to make a soft dough. This will take about 7 minutes.

3. Keep the dough for 30 minutes under a wet cloth till it doubles in volume.
4. Divide the dough into 5 equal portions and roll each portion into a circle of 150 mm. (6") diameter. Cut each circle into 5 equal triangles. Repeat with the remaining portions to make 20 more triangles.
5. Brush each triangle with a little oil and sprinkle some sesame seeds and poppy seeds on top.
6. Arrange these triangles on a greased baking tray and bake in a pre-heated oven at 180°C (360°F) for 10 minutes or till the chips turn golden brown.

Handy Tip: If you do not want to use the oven, just dry roast the dough triangles on a *tava* on both sides using a kitchen towel to flatten it as done for making khakhras.

✳ *Potato Wedges* ✳

Potato wedges coated with butter and spices, baked to crispiness and topped with cheese sprinklings.

Preparation time: 5 minutes.   Cooking time: 30 minutes.   Serves 4.
Baking temperature : 180°C (360°F).   Baking time : 30 to 35 minutes.

4 large potatoes cut into wedges (with the skin)
2 tbsp melted butter
2 cloves garlic, grated
½ tsp dried oregano
½ tsp dried rosemary
½ tsp crushed pepper
4 tbsp grated cheese
1 tbsp olive oil or oil
Salt to taste

1. Mix the melted butter, olive oil, garlic, oregano, rosemary, crushed pepper and salt in a bowl.

2. Add the potatoes and toss till the mixture coats the potatoes completely.
3. Place the potatoes in a baking tray in a single layer and bake in a pre-heated oven at 200°C (400°F) for 20 to 25 minutes or until the potatoes are cooked, stirring once in between.
4. Sprinkle cheese on top, mix well and bake for another 3 to 4 minutes.
   Serve immediately.

✲ *Jeera Kand Wafers* ✲

Yummy yam, crisped to perfection and flavoured with jeera powder.

Preparation time: 5 minutes.   Cooking time: Nil.   Makes 16 triangles.
Baking temperature : 150°C (300°F).   Baking time : 15 minutes.

2 cups peeled and thinly sliced *kand* (purple yam)
½ tsp roasted cumin seeds (*jeera*) powder
Salt to taste

1. Mix together the *kand,* cumin seeds powder and salt. Toss well.
2. Place the slices in a baking tray in a single layer.
3. Bake in an oven at 150°C (300°F) for 15 minutes or till crisp.
   Cool completely and store in an air-tight container.

✴ *Cheesy Bread Strips* ✴

Cheese and Tabasco sauce-coated bread slices crisped to perfection.

Preparation time: 5 minutes.   Cooking time: Nil.   Makes 20 strips.
Baking temperature : 180°C (360°F).   Baking time : 10 minutes.

4 whole wheat bread slices
½ cup cheese
Tabasco sauce for taste

1. Cut each bread slice into 5 thin strips to get 20 strips.
2. Combine the cheese with Tabasco sauce.
3. Apply this mixture on the bread strips and bake at 180°C (360°F) for about 10
   minutes. Serve immediately.

❋ *Fat Free Wafers* ❋

Worried about your waistline every time you reach out to fried stuff? Try these fat free wafers instead. Yes the microwave can indeed give you non-fried potato chips.

Preparation time: a few minutes.   Cooking time: 5-6 minutes.   Serves 4.

3 large potatoes, peeled
Salt and chilli powder to taste

1. Cut the potatoes into about 4 mm. thick slices.
2. Wash in cold water and dry thoroughly.
3. Arrange the potato slices in a microwave dish and microwave on HIGH for 5 to 6 minutes or until crisp.
4. Allow to cool. Store in an air-tight container.

Handy tip : You can use various vegetables like sweet potato, lotus stem etc. to make a variety of wafers.

✳ *Pita Chips* ✳

Pita bread spiced up with a coating of assorted spices, and baked to heavenly crispiness.

Preparation time: Nil.   Cooking time: Nil.   Makes varies as per the size of pita bread.   Baking temperature : 150°C (300°F).   Baking time : 10 minutes.

1 pita bread
2 tsp oil
2 tsp mixed herbs

1. Cut each pita bread into 1" thin long slices.
2. Sprinkle oil and herbs on the slices and bake in an oven at 150°C (300°F) for 15 minutes.
   Serve hot.

✳ *Baked Tortilla Chips* ✳

Here is an interesting way to make Tortilla chips with minimal oil. If you prefer the deep-fried kind, go ahead and indulge.

Preparation time: 5 minutes.   Cooking time: Nil.   Makes 20 tortilla chips.
Baking temperature : 190°C (380°F).   Baking time : 10 minutes.

¼ cup maize flour (*makai ka atta*)
¼ cup plain flour (*maida*)
1 tsp oil
Salt to taste
Plain flour *(maida)* for dusting

For garnish
Sesame seeds (*til*)

1. Combine all the ingredients in a bowl and knead into a soft dough using hot water.
2. Divide the dough into 6 equal portions.
3. Roll out each portion between two sheets of plastic into a thin circle of 175 mm. (7")
   diameter. Dust the tortillas generously with flour to make the rolling easier.

4. Lightly cook the tortillas on a non-stick pan.
5. Cut each tortilla into 6 triangular pieces.
6. Place the tortilla pieces in a single layer on a non-stick baking tray.
7. Bake at 190°C (380°F) for 7 to 8 minutes or until the tortilla chips are crisp and lightly browned.
8. Cool and store in an air-tight container.

Handy tip : Regular Tortilla chips are deep-fried. Follow a method you like.

BASIC RECIPES

＊ *Cream Cheese* ＊

Preparation time: a few minutes. Cooking time: 10 minutes. Makes 1½ cups.

1 litre full fat milk
1 tsp citric acid crystals
½ cup warm water

1. Put the milk to boil in a thick bottomed pan.
2. When it comes to a boil, remove from the flame and keep aside for a few minutes.
3. In another bowl, mix the citric acid crystals with the warm water.
4. Pour this mixture into the hot milk and allow to stand for about 5 minutes till the milk curdles on its own. Stir gently if required.
5. Strain this mixture using a muslin cloth.
6. Blend the drained milk solids in a food processor till smooth and creamy.

❋ *Sour Cream* ❋

Preparation time: 5 minutes.   Cooking time: Nil.   Makes 1½ cups.

200 grams fresh cream
1 to 2 tbsp thick curds (*dahi*)
2 pinches salt

1. Beat the cream until thick.
2. Add the curds and salt and mix well.

Handy tip : Use sour cream within 3 to 4 hours or make 2 to 3 hours prior to use.

Sun-dried Tomatoes

Makes ¾ cup (100 grams).

2 kg. firm red tomatoes
4 tablespoons sea salt (*khada namak*)

1. Wash and wipe the tomatoes.
2. Cut the tomatoes into quarters.
3. Toss the tomatoes with the salt, place on a sieve in a single layer and leave to dry under the sun.
4. When the sun sets, cover the sieve with a muslin cloth and bring it indoors.
5. Repeat for 6 to 7 days till the tomatoes dry out completely.
6. Store the sun-dried tomatoes in an air-tight container.

A magingazine by **TARLA DALAL**

Book your copy now...

Price : Rs. 50/-

SUBSCRIBE NOW & Get Free
Bonus Membership at tarladalal.com

Pick any one of the subscription offers and send us a cheque or a Demand Draft in favour of "Sanjay & Co." along with your detailed address including pin code, telephone no. and e-mail address.

Addressed to :

Sanjay & Co. 353, A-1, Shah & Nahar Industrial Estate, Dhanraj Mill Compound, Lower Parel (W), Mumbai 400013. INDIA

5 years (30 issues) + 1 Year Free Membership = Rs. 1450/-*

3 Years (18 issues) + 9 Months Free Membership = Rs. 1080/-*

1 Year (6 issues) + 2 Months Free Membership = Rs. 340/-*

*Offer valid for shipments only within India and is inclusive of shipping & handling charges.

For overseas shipments log on to tarladalal.com

For more information, call us on our helpline no. (022) 2496 8068 on all weekdays between 9.30 a.m. and 4.30 p.m. or write to us at subscription@tarladalal.com

Mini Series by *Tarla Dalal*

Healthy Breakfast

Healthy Snacks

Healthy
Soups & Salads

Healthy Juices

Fast Foods
Made Healthy

Calcium
Rich Recipes

Iron Rich Recipes

Forever Young Diet

Home Remedies

Low Cholesterol
Recipes